Jedidiah's Special Friend

A Faith Story

Copyright © 2021.

All rights reserved. No part of this book may be reproduced or used in any manner without the written permission of the copyright owner except for the use of quotations in a book review.

Written by Tomika Chance
Illustrated by Maruf Hasan

ISBN 979-8-9854415-0-5

Edited by BookBildr.com
Published by Agape Press

For my son,

may you continue to grow in the Lord and abide in His presence continually.

Hello, nice to meet you!
I'm Jedidiah.
And I want to tell you something, so would you please lend a listening ear and heart to me?

I have a very special friend living in my heart.
He is so dear to me.
Without Him, I could never be.

And even though I cannot see His face,
He's always there in my time of need.

He carefully put me together to
Create a unique boy like me.
So fairly and wonderfully made -
I'm His work of art, you see!

My friend is so awesome,
He makes my little heart sing.

I owe my life to my friend,
So I will praise Him eternally.

He loves me so much, even when I do not-so-good deeds.
He is forgiving and long-suffering, too.
He will never give up on me.
He washed away my sins and made me brand new.

Heaven has blessed me with a special friend,
Who I will walk with until the end.

He proved to me how he loves me
By giving His life on Calvary.

And He promised that one day
With Him in Heaven I will be.

He told all the grown-ups to suffer little
boys and girls to come unto Him.
We are not too young to sit and learn at His feet.

Whenever I need to talk to Him,
I get down on my knees and pray.
I can always trust that He
Will hear out every word I say.

I also read the Holy Bible
To know my friend much more.
It tells me of the gifts He has
For me in Heaven's store.

If I believe and love Him,
His blessings He will outpour.
A bright future for me He will ensure
If I keep knocking on heaven's door.

For I know the plans
I have for you,
declares the *Lord*,
plans to *prosper* you,
and not to harm you,
plans to give you
hope and a *future*.

Jeremiah 29:11

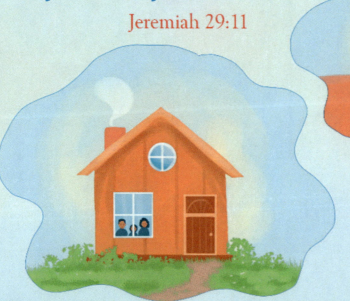

When I am sick and broken,
His pure touch makes me whole.
When I am sad, He makes me glad.
Oh, how He cheers me so.

I will hold his steady hands
And I will not let go.
His footsteps I will follow
To stand firm against the foe.

He said I'm to obey and honor my father and mother
Because it's right and I will be blessed all my life.

Ephesian 6:1-3

He teaches me not to be selfish
And to share Him with those I know.
His arms are wide open to receive you -
To Him you should joyfully go.

I will share my special friend with all the kids
So they will know
They too can have a trusted friend
To lean on wherever they may go.

His name is Jesus, the only Son of God,
King of Kings and Lord of Lords.
Oh, how I love Him so!

Jesus, I'm so happy you're my friend!

Then were there brought unto Him, little children, that He should put His hands on them, and pray: and the disciples rebuked them. And Jesus said, "Suffer, little children, and forbid them not, to come unto me: for such is the kingdom of heaven." And He laid His hands on them and departed thence.

Matthew 19:14-15

Made in the USA
Middletown, DE
29 July 2024